A Tax on My Love

For the person that felt like they couldn't

And then went on to do it.

A Tax on My Love
Toni Deshon

The loudest cry came from my
mother's tears,
This is proof that tears create
the most beautiful rainbows.
That tears are not a sign of
weakness but are signs of
growth.

The strongest fight came from
praying sisters,
This is proof that God answers
prayers.
That He listens even when you
think He hasn't heard you.

The imperfect man comes from
the existence of my father,

This is proof that even when you
think you aren't perfect,
You are perfect enough in
someone else's eyes.

The best listening came from an
empathetic aunt,
This is proof that God places
people in your life to help you
through what they have already
gone through.

The wisest words came from a
very dear friend.
This is proof that your truth can
help someone else step into their
own.

To my own little support system
that consist of parents, siblings,
friends and loved ones,
Thank you for unknowingly
molding me into the most
authentic version of myself

Preface:
Memory Lane

I remember like yesterday when I would stare at myself in the mirror and see absolutely nothing. I remember how I would speak so negatively about myself as if I deserved the way that I would treat me. I remember feeling for a person for the first time and giving my world to this person, but I could not even give my own world to me. Looking back at it, I realize how tough it was. I realize how not stupid or dumb or blindly in love, but how loveless I was when it came to loving me. Facing adversity with yourself is challenging. It is scary. It is boisterous in the time of loneliness and pain. It is soul snatching and spirit draining. It forms villains in heroes and storms in the presence of sunshine. However, saving myself only began when I made the decision and commitment to recreate and reconstruct myself. This compilation of spoken word poetry will, in hopes, console and inspire you in your time of healing. Let this collection encourage you in the occurrence of senseless thoughts and allow it to be medicine to the aches you have caused yourself by not truly loving you. Let these writings be a constant reminder that you have purpose and placement in the world we try our best to escape and allow it to help you find you in your season of uncertainty and absence of true love. I pray that this book blesses you and helps you in ways that are soulfully fulfilling and unimaginable.

-Toni Deshon

Opening Interlude

There was a funeral in the backyard of your soul the day you learn how to love yourself unconditionally and a delivery in a prayer room the morning after the old you died. You have learned how to love without conditions. You have learned how to love with a few boundaries intact. You have learned how to let your faith be greater than your fears and allow your heart to breathe without bleeding. You have learned to appreciate the parts of you that you would once lock up in the darkest closets of your soul and love the parts of you that you once wished did not contribute to the woman you have become—to the woman you are becoming. You have battled your insecurities with constant prayer and obedience as your power weapons. Your love has grown to be more than what you could ever fathom of it. You have exchanged generational curses for miraculous blessings. You are not any ordinary person. Your strength has given you a way to love wholeheartedly and not fear the risk in all things and people new. Everyday is not the best day but everyday is a blessing and a chance to be a better person than you were in yesterday's twenty-four hours, so this was written for you—to be a burial and not a resurrection, the seed of something phenomenal to soon manifests its presence in your life. I only hope that I remove the weeds of your intellect and replace them with fruitful harvests. That maybe, just maybe, you will learn to love yourself as much as I have learned to love myself and my ambition to teach you that even broken hearts can learn to love themselves as much as they have learned to love others.

Dear Self-----

I wondered who you'd be often, but I never took the true time to evaluate you. I blamed and I pointed the finger and I constantly complained about all that you weren't instead of appreciating who you were. I let you smile in the form of tears in the late-night, early mornings and cry in the form of smiles after the sun rose and before the sun set. I kept you hidden because I was afraid no one would see you. I was afraid that

your subtle soul and your utter
presence would attract to the
ones that meant you no good
and oppose those who brought
you joy in the most precious
form of morning. I chose to
neglect the truth of who you are
and run distances with lies that
never let you look back. I
became an off-brand version of
you—chasing dreams with
people but never chasing yours. I
chose to walk in the paths of
other people's purposes and
abandoned the importance of
what your calling meant to you.
God said my dear child I ask of

you to do this in love for me and I turned my back and pretended I never even heard His request. But then you said something to this off brand version of you and it resonated in the heart of who you truly were—you cannot half serve God and expect to be blessed abundantly. On that night, I chose to pivot. I chose to pivot, not into a three-sixty but into a one-eighty, because I desperately needed to find you and never return to the off brand that kept me imprisoned in its manipulative scheme of lies and deceit. And when the next morning came, I awaken in the purest version of you I'd ever examined.

The Urge to Quit in The Strength To Fight

I thought about quitting many times before but this time it had gotten a bit more complex. I was looking like a failure, smelling like a failure, walking like a failure, speaking like a failure. And those new Jordan's that I sported were all just a showcase of how my priorities were failing too.

My heart had felt that it could take all that it could take but see the beauty lied in the ability of my heart to heal itself and take the form it had naturally been born into. And my mind wasn't so sure on what to believe but all it did know was that it wanted to quit.

And so, I swallowed the pill that help me bypass these crazy thoughts and put my mind to rest. But even in my sleep I would dreams of all of the things I felt I could never have.
I would hear the you'll never be shit speeches and the why aren't you doing these things speeches

and my mind would become
their new but not so new victim.

To say the least, I forced me into
believing so poorly of myself so
frequently that my body and
spirit had followed suit. It had
fallen so beneath itself that when
I looked in the mirror tears
would stroke the sidewalks of
my skin.

I wanted to quit myself. I wanted
to quit life. I wanted to quit
everything that wanted me to
feel but I couldn't feel because

toxicity had taken its seat in everything that I had ever tried to find happiness, love and peace in. The urge to quit was at an all-time high and I was at my all-time low.

But in my low I found a peace and joy that this world could never snatch from me. They would throw their sticks. They would throw their stones. And I learned that it was those sticks and stones that had broken my bones, but it was my God's grace and mercy that always kept me. So yes, the urge to quit lived in

me but God, see, He was always
there to grab me and catch me
and love me and keep me and
lead me and that is why I never
threw in that towel.

Error: Love Lost

I thought finding love in you
would make me love me.
So, I held your approvals at my
hip.
I looked for your yes when
everyone would tell me no.
I looked for your comfort when
everyone would tell me to quit
crying.
I didn't realize how weak it was
making me.
I didn't realize how manipulative
it was until you walked away
knowing you were the only thing
that had my world spinning.

It forced me into a life I wasn't
ready to live without you.
It forced me into a deep hole that
I struggled to pull myself out of.
And just before I could say I
needed you, you showed me just
how much you didn't need me.
And in you showing me you
didn't need me, I found just how
much I needed myself.
So, I'm appreciative of you more
than I'd like to admit
And I thank you for proving to
me that not all disasters create
destruction.

What Ifs

I would wonder what you in my
life having more seriously would
have given me.
Would I have been hurt again?
Would I have been loved
properly?
Would I have spent my days
embracing the beauty of life with
a beautiful soul to share it with?
Would I have sold the last ounce
of my faith and fight to have you
stay at my side?

I am sorry that you never got the chance to witness this daring, witty love of mine.
I am sorry that the failure of others to love me properly scared me more than I would have loved to share a future with you.
I am sorry that I didn't love myself enough to accept that I deserved a love like you.
I am sorry for putting you through the similar things I, myself, had been put through

Please accept my apology in its purest, sincerest form.

Her Song

There was a song in the way that
she carried herself,
Poetry in the way she told her
heart's story.
The harmony of her poetry and
song were a bit strange.
They were not meant for one
another but flew together so
beautifully.

Disastrous Beauty

She was a beautiful disaster in
the season of springtime.
The eye of a tornado.
The waves of an earthquake that
shook every ground she ever
stepped foot on.
She was unpredictable and a
remembrance all in one.

Last Night

Last night I prayed for you because I had nothing left to give. You were sick of feeling sick and I was sick of watching you feel so sick of yourself that it struck a nerve in me to fall on my knees and talk to God about you. I just wanted you to see the love in you that I fell in love with and love the love in you that you were naively giving me.

Abandoned

I lay on the side of the bed that
you left abandoned by your
presence. I can smell the sweet
scent of your perfume. I can hear
the happiness in your calming
voice in the four walls of the
room that watched us make
memories too significant to
forget but too painful to
reminisce. I remember the times
when I could turn your late night
worries into my midnight
prayers while you lay asleep in
the comfort of my chest and I
remember when i felt that my

life wouldn't be worth enjoying
if i didn't have you to share it
with. I was at the gates of my
mustard seed of faith in love.
You were my mustard seed of
faith in love and just like any
other time, you failed me and
loving you hurt me.

Found

I found a strength in you that I didn't know I needed. I wanted to hate you. And to blame you. And to make you hurt how I was hurting but I only found a strength in you that I didn't know I needed in me. You taught me the rules to life in my pain of you walking away. And you taught me that my deepest fear was not loving me more than I loved and cherished anything else. And anyone else. And so I found a strength in you that I wasn't aware that I needed in me.

Because my tears of pain turned in my tears of Joy. And my tears of you turned into my love for her. And my tears because of them turned into my smiles despite them. And I just want to say thank you because I found a strength in you that I didn't know I needed. You taught me how to love the new entrances of people in my life and then embrace when it was their time to exit. You taught me how to appreciate silence. And appreciate falling. Because once upon a time my naive self was a bit too boisterous and too blind to my own uplifting. And now that I'm more quiet, I've learned more. And now that I'm keen, more observant, I see more. But I'm still appreciative to you because i found a strength in you that I didn't know I needed. And though when you chose to walk out of my life, it broke me to my core. Somehow, it strengthened me to walk in the light of how I deserved to be loved. And so i thank you for supplying me with the strength I needed to accept the fact that you would never deserve me and you would never love me how I'm supposed to be loved.   And thank you for exploiting the flaw in you so that I can gracefully leave my mark on the part of you that you'll so desperately crave when you realize you needed me way more than I ever needed you. And so the biggest strength that I ever found in you was walking away from the potential I saw in you and removing myself from the disappointments that your reality held. Because the strength that I found in you was how much I loved me.

Me or Them

I hate giving up but everyone I've ever encountered and walked away from made it easy for me to leave. They didn't value my presence, so I had to teach them of my absence. They didn't lose their pride and not once were they man enough or woman enough to simply and genuinely give an apology when they were wrong. I got tired of complaining about how I didn't feel loved enough or good enough because I was always the one being the bigger person or putting my pride aside because my relationships with them was more important to me than our disagreements and fall outs. I got tired of devaluing myself and my worth just to uphold theirs and so I learned how to leave my footprints where I could have still been for people that treated my love and respect for them as a toy . And I learned how to never feel guilty for loving and respecting myself more.

Letter to My Future Wife

I spend the beginning hours of my mornings talking to God about you. What you'd be like, the kind of woman you'd be to our kids and the kind of wife you'd be to me. I write letters to you and I write poetry about you and I spend my days preparing myself for the woman I asked God to quietly leave on the doorstep of my heart when he feels that I can handle all that could come with you. I wonder if you'd be involved in your community and if you'd be as caring and as daring and as loving and blissful as I am especially at the sound of love when our hearts speak each other's languages and our souls connect like puzzle pieces that were the missing pieces to the puzzles we always wanted to complete. I ask God to make me whole so that my whole can be more than enough for you on the days when you don't feel so whole yourself and that I'm able to carry you like he would carry us before he brought us to our intersection where love brought us together and where He kept us together and told us that we would be the missing parts to the fairytales we always dreamt of. I dream of all that you are and all that you'll be and i pray over the woman that lives inside of you because that is the woman who I'll marry someday and the woman I will fall for and thank God for blessing me with.

Fairytale Love

You damn near killed me the day
you chose her over me. To love
her, treat her, spoil her, and feed
her. I wanted to be held at night
in the arms of your comfort. I
wanted to be loved like how
Darius loved Nina and how
Andre loved Sidney. I wanted
bubble baths and candlelit
dinners and parked car
conversations and even those
cute little Goodmorning and
goodnight messages that you
would send her to go to sleep to

and wake up to. I wanted to experience the butterflies in my tummy and chills down my arms and spine when our bodies greeted each other more personally. I wanted musical playlists specifically made for me by you and I wanted picnics and walks in the park under the stars. I wanted love and not attachment. I wanted mistakes and growth from them and not perfection. I wanted a love without conditions, and I wanted a woman and not a girl. A warrior and not a worrier. A gentle soul and not a bitter

spirit. And when I stopped
expecting so much from people
I didn't need, I received
everything and everyone that I
would once upon a time
overlook or under appreciate.
So, I appreciate you for teaching
me that fairytale loves only exist
in movies.

The Dumbest Thing We Ever Shared

I pushed love on you beyond the limits you could handle and it self-destructed right in my face. I wanted us to last but you would always put me last and now our last has come down to the thick of your pride and my unapologetic ego and we're ready to risk everything we ever built because we do not want to feel like the weaker being in our union and that is the dumbest thing that we've ever shared.

Love on Fear Street

I am not afraid of love and all
that it can bring, take and reveal.
I am afraid of getting my hopes
up just for them to be shot down.
I am afraid of sharing my love
only to be taken for granted. I
am afraid of feeling lonely in a
bed, in a room, in a space, in my
solitude when I am supposed to
have someone there who is
supposed to be the one who I
share these things with. I am not
afraid of love, but perhaps the
risk that one has to be willing to
take. Or even the slightest

measure of uncertainty in a person's heart that they won't reveal for their own selfish gain. I am afraid that no one will love me enough to be honest and open with me about their intentions, thoughts, and emotions. I am afraid of being half loved and half wanted. I am afraid of being under appreciated. I am afraid of being hurt by the one person I put my trust in to never hurt me. I am not afraid of love, I am afraid of how others perceive love and how unimportant it is to them.

Traffic Lights

I waited for the green light when
you would finally give me a go.
Not a proceed with caution.
Not a stop. Not a green or yellow
light to direct me left or right.
But a go. I patiently waited on
the go that my gut felt you would
never give me.

Cheers to My Twenty Somethings

I spent the early years of my twenty somethings trying to figure me out. My life completely dismantled itself and I felt lost for a bit. Betrayed. Failed. Empty. Shattered. I felt uncomfortable around my friends because I felt like I no longer served any purpose in their lives. And I felt unworthy when I was around family because I felt that I was the disappointment child—and granddaughter—and niece—and cousin—and sibling. I felt that I wasn't enough to the ones who were more than enough for me. And so, I searched to fill my voids of the way I wanted to be loved by giving the love I desperately wanted out freely but so harmfully until I was able to face and admit my insecurities and unpleasant behaviors. I realized I was afraid of first acknowledging me—and my faults—and my own transgressions. I was afraid of having to change and admit that I was the toxic person in some peoples' lives. I could not stomach that thought of knowing I'd possibly hurt people that only wanted the best for me because I was hurting in ways I could not accept I was hurting—and it pushed some away. It caused some to give up on me. It caused some to walk away. It caused some to turn their blind eye and pretend that they weren't seeing me self-destruct. But I have come to learn that my twenty somethings are only the building blocks of this journey called adulthood. It is the years we call our foundations—and I had to rebuild my foundation because I could not allow the tactics of the generational curses I'd been born into win. I could not allow my foundation to be built on the weaknesses of the two families that intertwined to create the breath of life in me, so I chose to change my perception—and change my mindset—and it has changed my life for the better.

Cravings

I crave a love of purity & genuineness. A love I never have to question. A love I never have to cry tears of sadness for. A love that uplifts & teaches me and not belittles & breaks me. I crave a love that never hides me and never keeps me a secret. A love that kisses me awake in the morning and pleasurably puts me to sleep at night. I crave a love that takes me out for coffee in the mornings just to get to know me better and not a love that takes me out at night just to look forward to a "nightcap". I crave a love that lands me at an alter exchanging vows and the words I do in front of both our families &friends. I crave a love that blesses me with a family because kids are truly the most precious gifts God can give. I crave a love that has a foundation built with His strength & His love. I crave a love that knows no bounds and it forever grows. I crave a love that welcomes change and not a love that fears it. I crave a love that knows how to apologize and a love that knows how to admit it is falling apart. I crave a love that wants my assistance and appreciates my perceptive of things blind to its eye. I crave a love that knows the worth in compromising so that we never let it die. I crave a love in the form of smiles but can handle the art of tears too. I crave a love that accept, acknowledges and admits all of the wrongs they will sometimes do.

The Art of Embracing

I am learning to love the parts of me that I abandoned because of the inadequate opinions of the pernicious people I allowed to validate its necessity in my life. I am growing in love with who I am and not who others have always made me to be. I choose to embrace the flaws that have given me peace in knowing that perfection is nonexistent, and I am more than enough for the people purposely meant for me.

A Prayer for Tonisia Deshon

I pray someday that true love finds you and shows you well. And that you find peace and comfort in God's love above all else. I pray that your happiness becomes founded on the elements you were once too afraid to welcome and that your foundation disperses those elements that caused chaos in your mind and were deceiving of who you always were. I pray for a 1 Corinthians 13 woman and a Proverbs 31 woman to manifest her presence in the woman you're becoming—and I pray you do not scrutinize your character when people fail to accept you for how you come. I pray for your wisdom and your discernment—to know when someone or something is for you—and that you feel it in the pit of your stomach when they are not. I pray that you know the difference between love and lies and the difference between effort and indolence. I pray for your well-being your strength—the essence of who you will be—and all the world will see.

The Power of Heartbreak

I don't think that people understand the real power that heartbreak has on those that have their hearts broken by people. When you break a heart, you do not only break that. You destroy a soul. You destroy a person's ability to ever trust again, to ever open up again, to ever see their true worth and value again because now that person lives with the questions, "Why wasn't I good enough? Why wasn't I important enough? How do I cope with things when everything reminds me of him/her? and sometimes Why them?" And that hurts because when the right person finally comes along, they are the ones who suffer the consequences of your actions. They are the ones who must try their very best to heal a broken soul that they didn't break all while trying not to lose themselves in the process. So, if you don't love someone, do not lead them on. Walk away when your feelings start to change and when you know you don't have good intentions. Do not be selfish because the pain that you will cause by walking away cannot compare and will never compare to the pain you will cause by leading a person on, misusing them, or abusing the love that they will give . On the other hand, especially, do not enter a serious relationship if you're not ready for the commitment, if you're not ready for the bad times and hard times, if you're not ready to allow the next person to restore what another has shattered & broken. Most importantly do not enter a serious relationship if you are not ready to add value to a person's life and value to the relationship.

This Mess I Made

I hope this does for you what it has done for me. Ya see, my life went into a whirlwind the day we called it quits. Seeing you with those other women ate my flesh completely. I had run out of options on how to steer you back to me. My head and my heart were at a crossroad. I shaped you into the best way and you shaped me into the worst way. I became numb and empty and couldn't control any of my feelings. My anger was at an all-time high with you. My life wouldn't move forward without the part that included you. However, one day a woman came into my life and she held me so closely and a depiction of my life completed was painted so vividly into my head. It terrified me. I ran. I couldn't stomach the thought of someone coming in and restoring the piece of me you left to die. I pushed the blessing that I'd been praying for so hard right into someone else's arms. But see now, my pain is caused still because of you. My fear and my insecurities from our relationship was the control button that kept me from a peace and happiness I desperately craved to have. Now I'm watching my blessing try to love a person not meant for her like I was and it's hard trying not to intervene. It's hard to see her cry or upset because of a person I pushed her into choosing over me. I pray God can fix this mess i made. I pray the woman I'm loving afar now will see better days.

Feeling Everything,
While Feeling Nothing

You stole something from me that day in the midst of our irreplaceable smiles and unapologetic laughs. My heart had escaped the security of my rib cage and into the palm of your hands and I'd never been so afraid yet anxious for a result until that moment. Your beautiful brown eyes, ya see, they told a story I was familiar with, but my soul rejoiced at the feel of your embrace. and my mind? Well, it craved you on a level that was new to me. I was truly happy. I did everything in my power to keep you around because letting you stray would have meant losing a prized possession that had my name written all over it, my heart. I compromised things to keep you around. I gave up things I'd work for to keep that same smile. I even compromised me just to be enough for you. But I wasn't. You kept me around through your caterpillar and cocoon stage and before you blossomed into this breathtaking butterfly, you dropped me like a basketball, expecting me to deflect when you were ready to love me again. But that ball, the ball you considered me. See, it was flat. So, when you dropped me, I never deflected and I was forced to watch you give another person everything I created in you, everything I molded you into. It was painful. Like IP painful. I died alive watching you love another while I was still loving you. And when you finally picked me up and realized I was flat; I was torn into pieces. So here we are now and you're expecting me to love you no differently. But how do I get passed you breaking every piece of my heart? How do I even get back to living and doing my part?

Murder She Wrote

I wrote a love letter for you in the form of a dying wish. Of all of the things I never got to say to you because fear wouldn't let me speak but love would let me write. So many I won't nothing to do with yous that you mistook my fear of loving you for my decision to destroy you. It broke your heart to not have me like you wanted but it would have broken my soul if I would've given you me without fully loving myself first. I wanted to feel your happiness. You were my peace. But I couldn't be selfish and bring you into the chaos that lived in the clouds of my thoughts and the slander against myself that would sneak out my head like thieves in the night. Your aura was to me what an air vent is to a prisoner serving life without parole: hope. But see having hope wasn't the same as having faith. I was expecting that healing to happen or come instead of knowing and believing that through God it would. I would watch you through the lenses of life and adore the trails of gold you would leave behind after you planted your feet along the divergent paths you took. Your light gave the strength of the sun a fight because even without the sun you lit up my world. And baby I just want you to know that though you never got the chance to show me the love you had to offer you changed my life and made me whole. So, to the love of my life I never got to experience. I'm sorry because denying your love was a Murder that I Wrote.

Take Me Back

I keep replaying the situation back in my head and my heart won't heal from the pain of that night. To feel so alone in a world full of human companions and none of them can see through the mask I wear. I've tried being strong when all I've felt was weak. I've tried to move on when all I've wanted was revenge. In a ring fighting my forgiveness against my anger and my forgiveness putting up a good fight but my anger man it's still winning. Hiding my pain from the ones that matter to me, trying stay the course after eyeing that beast of a storm. Sleepless nights in the arms of someone I barely even know. Telling all my worries to a person I know will always judge and never understand. And the pain it's getting unbearable, I can feel the fist prints and boot prints of the ones that abused my love or walked out on me. Lost and confused struggling to find my way and redevelop the peace that I once had, so tell me what is it that the enemy want. Because I have nothing my cup has been emptied. I'm drained by heartbreaks and heartaches and invisibility. Sucked dry by lies and misinterpretations and abuse mentally and emotionally. Tell me what a person like I suppose to do. Do I give up or do I keep fighting? Do I say something, or do I continue to hide it? Damn, I miss the times when I didn't have stress. When I was happy all of the time and I was at my best. Take me back to the days I was a kid. Please Lord, take me back to the happiness I had in my childhood.

Let's Love

I wish I would have loved you like I know I'm capable of instead of pushing you away. You were everything I knew I wanted and needed. But I was too afraid and too stuck in belief that you could possibly turn out to be everyone else that I didn't accept your brand of love. I didn't accept your brand of loyalty and real because I didn't believe that great people exist and that you could have restored me until I watched you swaddle another in your arms like a mother would do her child.

That feeling of security, you know the times i got to feel your embrace. It would sing a melody to my heart but would create a diss song in my mind because I was torn between letting you love me or watching you slowly slip out of my life overtime. So, because of my brokenness and because of my lack of making good choices for myself I'm stuck hoping that someday you'll understand that I love you. That someday you'll realize that I'm gracefully broken with a heart afraid of being loved because whenever it gets its hopes up at any feeling of happiness it's quickly snatched away. That someday I'll get the opportunity to show you what loving me truly would have gotten you because I'm sick of playing the mind games and the hurt me before I hurt you games with other girls that don't deserve me. And I'm sick of rejecting you because I fear so many things that are good for me and to me and I'm done with questioning whether I deserve you. Because I know that I do. Come. Take my hand. Let's do something others failed to do. Let's love each other.

Desire the love you have shown
and given others as a love you
want for yourself and then give it
to her in a way that surpasses
the grounds you allowed abuse to
walk along.

Give yourself time to heal.
Do not dwell on the bumps in life
that sometimes shatter our
hearts but never stops its
beating.
Give yourself a chance.
Just breathe.

Postface:
A Look into My Present

I once let fear write the plan for my life—like not expressing what I was feeling. I allowed the days to bypass me because I was hating the lie I was living. I didn't go after any opportunities because I would let my denials and fear of setbacks take control of my thinking. It was myself that I was once fearing. I was existing and never living. I was never risking but always feeling. I would never step out of the comfort zone that would keep me trapped away from my potential. I didn't believe I had it in me. I couldn't see what others saw because everything they saw as beauty was everything I saw as a flaw, but the day eventually came in the time of my lowest. It was in my greatest loss that I discovered my God-sent purpose.

-Toni Deshon

A Tax on My Love